Extraordinary Girls

United States

To my grandmothers, *dadiji* and *naniji,* and my
mother, Rooplata Ajmera—*Maya*

To my sisters, Abidemi, Omolola, Asisat,
Bilikis, and Vonette—*Teju*

To my "little sister" and friend, Qua-Neta,
and my niece, Elizabeth—*Sarah*

Kenya

United States

Extraordinary
Girls

Maya Ajmera • Olateju Omolodun
Sarah Strunk

with a foreword by Isabel Carter Stewart of *Girls Incorporated*®

Russia

SHAKTI for Children

Charlesbridge

Intense

Bold

Hardworking

Talented

Energetic

Focused

Feisty

Beautiful

Generous

Intelligent

Inspiring

Daring

Independent

Adventurous

Insightful

Athletic

Motivated

Spunky

Dynamic

Innovative

Spiritual

Thoughtful

Wise

Fierce

Goofy

Amazing

Sensitive

Contents

Foreword

The eldest daughter who watches over her siblings, the little sister who wishes she could grow up faster, the circle of girlfriends who whisper to each other and then break into fits of laughter—each girl is extraordinary in her own way; each has something to celebrate.

United States

All girls have unique personalities, experiences, and aspirations that make up who they are and how they view the world. *Extraordinary Girls* affirms that individuality, celebrating girls' diversity while never losing sight of the many things they share. It captures the fortitude, bravery, and ingenuity of girls.

It is my pleasure to lead Girls Incorporated, the organization that inspires girls to be "strong, smart, and bold." But more often I find that it is the girls who inspire us. And, most of all, it is the girls who inspire one another. Girls are community activists and religious leaders, artists and performers, athletes and intellectuals, confidantes and friends. Though the outlets for these energies vary from country to country, the creative spirit and dynamism with which girls around the world express themselves set a strong, smart, and bold example for others to follow.

Kyrgyzstan

As an educator and advocate for the rights of girls, I have learned that when we support and respect girls as individuals, as members of communities, and as part of a global society, girls respond by trusting their own voices as they become their own best advocates. The result is truly extraordinary.

Isabel Carter Stewart
National Executive Director
Girls Incorporated®

India

To Be a Girl

Every girl is unique. Are you tall or short? Are you dark, light, or some shade in between? Are you artistic or scientific, reflective or outgoing? These characteristics make you an individual, but all girls have a lot in common. Girls are strong and smart. Girls are caring and compassionate. And girls are creative and curious.

United States

Girls are making a difference every day. They are taking a stand against violence. They are helping to save the environment, training to become world-class athletes, and championing for peace. Ordinary girls have extraordinary abilities. With hard work and determination, support from their families and communities, and a little bit of luck, girls can do anything!

Bangladesh

Bolivia

Guatemala

Mozambique

The most important person in your life is you. Being a girl is not always easy, and you will face many challenges as you grow up. Be true to yourself by taking care of your body and your mind. Don't let the media influence how you look, feel, or act. Question the images you see on television and in magazines. Sleep well, eat healthy foods, exercise, and most of all, feel good about yourself.

China

No matter how young or old you are, you can always keep growing! Celebrate your heritage and become a lifelong learner. Be an adventurer, meet challenges head-on, and share your accomplishments with others. Pursue your dreams and be your own best friend. Be proud that you're a girl!

Canada

United States

Different Ways to Learn

Learning can happen anywhere. Girls have different opportunities for learning, and they learn in different ways and in different places. Going on a field trip, volunteering, inventing a gadget, or visiting a zoo are all opportunities for learning. Girls can also learn by reading books, surfing the World Wide Web, and having hobbies, but the most common place they learn is at school.

United States

Girls are hard workers. They can complete any school assignment, from conducting science experiments to solving difficult math problems to creating beautiful collages for art class. In or out of school, girls may learn about accomplished women like Marie Curie, the chemist and physicist who discovered radium and polonium. They might read stories by Judy Blume. Or they might find out about important warriors like Joan of Arc, Nobel Peace Prize winners like Aung San Suu Kyi, or enterprising businesswomen like Madame C. J. Walker.

Vietnam

Canada

Nigeria

Mexico

Jody-Anne

Girls are smart. They enter, participate in, and win many academic competitions. In 1998 twelve-year-old Jody-Anne Maxwell, from Jamaica, won the Scripps Howard National Spelling Bee. She was the first non-United States citizen to win this contest. She spelled words like *daedal* (intricate) and *hyssop* (an aromatic plant). She outspelled 248 other finalists to spell c*hiaroscurist* (an artist who emphasizes the contrasts between light and dark). Jody-Anne says that "God and training" helped her win.

Jody-Anne Maxwell

Beth Peres

Beth

Girls are assertive. At age ten Beth Peres, of the United States, wanted her parents to increase her weekly allowance. She was not sure how much to ask for so she surveyed her classmates. She discovered that the boys averaged $3.18 per week, while the girls earned only $2.63—even though girls reported doing four times as many chores as boys. Beth says, "It's not fair. Girls should get paid as much as boys, or more when they do more work." Her findings were reported in the *Wall Street Journal,* the *Washington Post,* and many other newspapers.

Alexis Brown

Alexis

Girls learn by using technology. Alexis Brown, of the United States, is a publisher and a Webmaster. She was just ten years old when she started the Kids' Hospital Network. This network supports sick kids all over the world through a newsletter called *Bearable Times,* a Web site, scholarships, kids' clubs, and other programs. Alexis describes herself as "an advocate for kids helping other kids." She believes that you can accomplish just about anything you set your mind to.

Seeds of Peace campers

Manal and Shirley, campers from Jordan and Israel

Seeds of Peace

Girls learn from others. Girls have strong opinions and are not afraid to share their points of view. At the Seeds of Peace International Camp in the United States, Jordanians, Israelis, Palestinians, Egyptians, and other young people from Middle Eastern countries come together to talk about how they can build a bridge for peace. At the camp, girls and boys learn how to develop their own opinions rather than just accepting those of their governments. By learning about each other, they develop strong friendships that overcome political barriers.

Mayerly

Girls are leaders. Colombian girls have been doing their part to teach children and adults to end violence in their country through the Children's Mandate for Peace, Life, and Freedom. By the time she was thirteen, one of these activists, Mayerly Sanchez, had appeared on television and radio and in newspapers to encourage Colombian children to think and act for peace. She is a role model for girls everywhere, showing them that their voices can be heard and their dreams realized. For their work, Mayerly and the children of Colombia were nominated for the 1998 Nobel Peace Prize.

Mayerly Sanchez, right

Larissa Vingilis-Jaremko

Larissa

Girls are scientific. At age nine Larissa Vingilis-Jaremko founded a club called the Canadian Association for Girls in Science (CAGIS) to inspire girls to love science. CAGIS has several branches across Canada, and every month girls take field trips to meet different female scientists, such as an archaeologist and a neuropsychologist. The CAGIS Web site has given girls around the world the opportunity to become virtual members. Larissa says, "I really wanted to erase the stereotypes many girls had about scientists being geeky old men with big glasses. Any girl can grow up to be a scientist."

Michelle Tees

Michelle

Girls are entrepreneurial. Michelle Tees, from the United States, started her own business at age nine. She sold different types of plants, including geraniums, impatiens, and vegetables. Her company, Michelle's Greenhouses, became so successful that she soon had eight greenhouses. She tended to the plants with the help of her family after school, on weekends, and during the summer. In her small business Michelle learned about money management, problem solving, and the importance of hard work. Michelle says, "It is important for girls to find something they love to do, to ask questions, and to keep learning every day."

United States

Girls are resilient. For many girls, education is a dream. They may receive very little schooling or no schooling at all. There are several reasons why girls don't receive a good education, but the most common reason is poverty. Some girls must work at a young age to help support their families. Others may be in charge of growing food and preparing their families' meals. In some places girls are not valued as highly as boys. Some girls marry at an early age and may not complete their studies. Despite these challenges, many girls are finding ways to balance education and their other responsibilities.

Israel

Cambodia

Pakistan

Russia

Guatemala

Lucia Punungwe, right

Lucia

Education is a human right for all girls. Organizations in many countries have started schools and educational programs for girls. The Cambridge Female Education Trust (CamFed) in the United Kingdom is helping girls in Zimbabwe and Ghana obtain educations by paying for their school fees, uniforms, and other items. When she was fifteen, Lucia Punungwe, from Zimbabwe, spoke to parliamentarians in the United Kingdom about how education has changed her life. "Knowledge is power! I can start money-generating projects using the knowledge I get from school. I am going to serve as a role model in my community. Education has increased my creativity and intelligence."

Making a Difference

Girls are powerful. They are activists who work to ease the problems of poverty, homelessness, pollution, illiteracy, and illness. Girls Incorporated, Girl Scouts, Pioneer Girls, 4-H, and Habitat for Humanity are just some of the organizations through which girls contribute to society. In South Africa, China, Belarus, and many other countries, girls proudly wear the uniforms of their service organizations.

Colombia

Belarus

Mexico

Girls are independent. You don't need to belong to an organization to help your community. You can volunteer at a hospital and read to the patients. You can write letters to your government representatives or your local newspaper to express your opinions. You can participate in athletic events that support the fight against AIDS or the search for a cure for breast cancer.

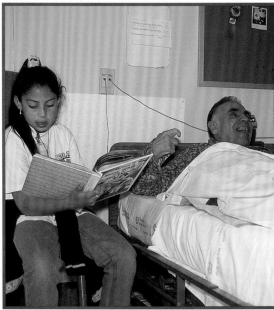

United States

Arlys Endres

Arlys

Girls are successful fund-raisers. When she was ten years old, Arlys Endres, from the United States, became an advocate for "herstory"—the stories of women like Susan B. Anthony, who fought for women's rights in the United States. Arlys joined the Susan B. Anthony Campaign to help reinstall a statue of Anthony and two other feminists in the Rotunda, the central area of the United States Capitol. She wrote letters to more than 2,000 people asking them to donate Susan B. Anthony coins or dollar bills with *Susan B. Anthony* written on them. She raised almost $2,000, and her hard work paid off when Congress voted to return the statue to the Rotunda. Arlys says, "It was important to fight for Susan B. Anthony's rights because she fought for mine."

Patricia

Girls are courageous. From the time she was ten years old, Patricia Cruzado has been helping to end abuses of child labor in Peru. By age fifteen she had become a leader in the national child-worker movement by speaking to government and community leaders. Many girls around the world work long hours in unsafe jobs that do not provide fair wages or health care. Some countries do not have laws to protect children who work for pay. Patricia opposes dangerous work and believes that children need work with dignity to help their families and to pay school costs.

Patricia Cruzado

Kory Johnson

Kory

Girls are visionaries. Kory Johnson, of the United States, became an environmental activist when she was nine years old. She organized other children to protest against industrial pollution and founded the grassroots environmental group Children for a Safe Environment. She battled against governments and businesses that build environmentally hazardous facilities, often where society's poorest people live. In 1998 she was the youngest person ever to win the prestigious $100,000 Goldman Environmental Prize. Kory says, "I want other girls to know that it doesn't matter whether you are rich or poor; every girl can make a difference."

Ethiopia

Girls are environmentalists. They are planting new trees in Ethiopia, Kenya, India, and other countries. They are not only saving forests, they are saving animals, too. In Vestmannaeyjar, Iceland, girls and boys work together to rescue seabirds called puffins. Starting recycling programs, picking up litter, planting an urban garden, and protecting rivers are just some of the other ways girls can be environmentalists.

Iceland

Aubyn Burnside

Aubyn

Girls are mobilizers. When Aubyn Burnside, of the United States, was eleven years old, she learned that foster children often move from home to home carrying their belongings in garbage bags. To help, Aubyn established Suitcases for Kids. She organized scout troops, 4-H clubs, and church groups to donate suitcases to foster children. Aubyn hoped to collect 200 pieces of luggage. She not only met her goal, she exceeded it by collecting more than 10,000 suitcases. Through chapters started by other children, Suitcases for Kids spread from North Carolina across the United States. Aubyn says, "Whatever you dream of doing, age should not keep you from achieving your goals."

China

Indonesia

Girls are networkers. In 1998 fifteen girls from nine countries—Armenia, Brazil, Chile, The Gambia, Malaysia, Nepal, Singapore, the United Kingdom, and the United States—came together for "Speak Out!", a forum presented at the United Nations by the International Network for Girls. This forum provided an opportunity for these girls to share the joys and challenges of their girlhoods. Not only did they learn from each other, they demonstrated how girls can be effective agents for change.

Girls are dreamers and doers. They know that it's not enough to have great ideas—they must also make them happen. Girls are risk takers, and they recognize the power they have to change their world.

United Kingdom

19

Religion and Spirituality

Religion and spirituality are important parts of many girls' lives. Girls may read the Holy Bible, the Torah, the Book of Mormon, the Bhagavad Gita, the Qur'an, or other religious texts. They may express their spirituality in many settings, such as a church, a home, a mosque, the outdoors, a synagogue, or a temple. There are many different religions and faiths in the world. While their specific observances, symbols, and beliefs are unique, they share common threads.

Egypt

Indonesia

India

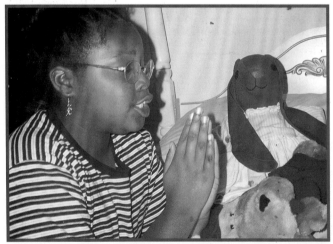

United States

Prayer, a part of most religions, is practiced in many ways. You may pray by clasping your hands together, bowing your head, and closing your eyes. You may pray by yourself or with others, silently or out loud. Hindu and Jain girls pray around candles and incense in a ceremony called *puja*. Muslim girls are taught to pray five times a day. They place a prayer mat facing the holy city of Mecca and pray to Allah, or God. Many Christian girls pray at mealtime or at bedtime, giving thanks and asking God to care for their families, friends, and others around the world.

Philippines

Sometimes you can tell a girl's religion from what she wears. Girls who cover their heads with scarves may belong to the Islamic faith. Some girls wear crosses to proclaim their Christian faith, while some Jewish girls wear the Star of David. Some Buddhist girls devote their lives to the Buddha by becoming nuns. They wear robes and shave their heads, much as the Buddha did. In many religions girls can grow up to become rabbis, nuns, priests, or ministers.

Goddesses are very important in many religions. Some girls pray to them to ensure health, a good harvest, and many other things. In Hinduism an important goddess is Shakti, who symbolizes strength and wisdom. Oya, the goddess of female leadership, is worshipped by the Yoruba people of Nigeria. They admire her skill with words and ask for her help in resolving conflicts.

Peru

Myanmar

United States

Nepal

United States

Most Native American spiritual traditions emphasize that the earth is alive and a source of life. Many Native American girls maintain a strong connection to Mother Earth through prayer, ceremonies, storytelling, songs, and dance. When an Apache girl reaches adolescence, she is honored with a four-day ceremony. Friends and family help her celebrate the transition from girlhood to womanhood. After this event the young woman becomes a role model for younger girls.

Ireland

Rites of passage are important to many girls. Some Jewish communities hold a special ceremony called a bat mitzvah for Jewish girls, usually on the first Friday before the girl's thirteenth birthday. She reads aloud from the Torah, a Jewish holy text, and makes a commitment to lead a Jewish life. First Communion and confirmation are important events in the lives of many Christian girls. Most Roman Catholic girls receive the Eucharist, or Holy Communion, for the first time around age eight. In some Protestant churches girls attend religious classes around age twelve or thirteen and then participate in a confirmation ceremony. As with a bat mitzvah and a first Communion, family and friends may gather afterward for a celebration.

United States

Festivals and holidays are celebrated around the world to honor religious occasions. Some of the major religious holidays are Christmas in Christianity, Rosh Hashanah in Judaism, Eid al-Fitr in Islam, and Diwali in Hinduism. During these holidays and throughout the year, many girls and their families try to help those who are less fortunate than they are. Making a difference in the lives of others is an important part of most religions. Mother Teresa, a Catholic nun and crusader for the poor, devoted her life to helping the sick and impoverished, no matter what their religion. Her selfless and inspiring work made her a role model for girls everywhere.

Colombia

Mexico

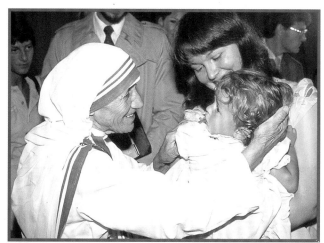
United States

Laos

The Arts

Girls have an artistic spirit. Art can move you to laugh, cry, shout, or gaze in wonder. You can express your artistic side by being an actor or writer, painter or sculptor, quilter or designer, dancer or musician.

Girls are dynamic. Rotating hips, elegant hand movements, tapping feet, and leaping bodies can express joy or sorrow. All over the world, dances are performed to celebrate cultural or religious occasions. Many girls in Russia study ballet, while in India some girls learn Manipuri dance. Jazz, tap, ballet, lyrical dance, and hip-hop are popular in North America and in many European countries. Girls also dance at parties, with their friends, and to songs on the radio.

Russia

China

Ghana

India

Lebanon

Lindy Gibbons

Lindy

Girls are graceful. Lindy Gibbons, from the United States, started dancing at age three and has won medals in jazz, tap, ballet, and lyrical dance. When she was thirteen Lindy won second place for a dance she choreographed and performed in the national "I Love Dance" student choreography competition. To girls interested in dance Lindy says, "Anyone can do it; you just have to be open." Even though she is a professional dancer and performs for large audiences, to Lindy dancing is also a natural art that can be done just for fun. Lindy will keep dancing as she grows older, but she also enjoys science and math, and she dreams of becoming an engineer one day.

Grenada

Indonesia

United Kingdom

Girls are musical. Some girls can beat the drums with energy, play the violin with elegance, or pluck the sitar with passion. Others are just learning to play instruments, such as the bagpipes, cello, or harp. Girls may play in an orchestra at school or march in a band at parades and community festivals. They can use almost anything to make music, from tapping feet to clapping hands to shaking pebbles to clinking soda bottles.

Girls Choir of Harlem

Girls are committed. Choir, theater, and dance require girls to practice together frequently. Members of the Girls Choir of Harlem rehearse every day to prepare for performances and improve their skills. They attend the Choir Academy of Harlem, where they study music as part of their education. After their first year at the school, they attend a summer camp where they practice, practice, and practice. Spending time together helps the girls build team spirit. Choir members agree that music is a language; it is the way they express themselves as sisters. The friendships they share support every member of the group.

Girls Choir of Harlem

Alexandra

Alexandra Nechita

Girls are expressive. Painters, sculptors, and other visual artists share their feelings through their work. Romanian-born painter Alexandra Nechita has been painting since she was four. She says she tries to express something special in each of her paintings. A self-taught artist, Alexandra creates abstract pieces. By age eleven she had published a book of her work, called *Outside the Lines*. Alexandra says, "No child should be deprived of their right and opportunity to express themselves."

Peace Collector by Alexandra Nechita

Armenia

United States

Girls are eloquent. Some girls are writers, poets, or storytellers and use language in enchanting ways. Their words can take their audience on a journey to an ancient place or on a mysterious adventure. You may begin writing by doing it just for yourself. You may keep a diary to record your feelings and thoughts like Anne Frank, who wrote about her experiences during the Holocaust. Her journal was later published as *Anne Frank: The Diary of a Young Girl,* which has been read by girls all over the world.

Alex

Girls are creative. Some girls publish their work in magazines, newspapers, and on the Internet so that they can share their voices with others. When she was eight years old, Alex Whitney, of the United States, wrote and illustrated *Mouse Surprise,* a book about a family of mice that creates a birthday surprise for a cat. She won a national contest for stories written and illustrated by students, and her book was published. Maybe you are a writer like Alex and dream of becoming a famous novelist like Nobel Prize winner Toni Morrison.

Alex Whitney

Eritrea

United States

Girls appreciate beauty. They discover natural forms of art all around them. A hula dancer in the Hawaiian Islands may wear leis made of ferns and flowers as she dances to a song that tells the story of Pele, the goddess of the volcano. For weddings and other special occasions in India, Oman, and many other countries, girls decorate their hands with henna, a dye that comes from the leaves of a small shrub. All over the world girls may string wildflowers together to create glorious crowns.

Ecuador

Oman

28

Guatemala

Girls have style. You may reveal your artistic spirit in your clothing, hairstyle, and jewelry. You might have a favorite pair of jeans or shoes, or a dress that makes you feel great when you put it on. Or you may adorn yourself like a beautiful work of art by wearing flowers, feathers, or beads. Other ways of dressing up can be more elaborate. Some girls can sew or weave and make their own clothes or beautiful blankets for their families.

United States

Germany

Girls are talented. Creating a work of art can let you express your feelings about yourself; your friends, family, and community; or the world around you. You can choose to share your art with others or to keep it private. Your creativity can be an act of self-expression that nourishes the spirit.

Slovakia

Indonesia

Sports and Play

Girls are playful. Play energizes the spirit, the body, and the mind. You can play alone, with a small group of friends, or on an organized team. You can play inside or outside. Some types of play require concentration or an active imagination, while others rely on physical fitness and agility. All types of play can teach you about having fun, making friends, and building new skills.

Girls are imaginative. They can think of hundreds of ways to play. They might imagine themselves driving a race car across the finish line or hosting a tea party with their friends. They may invent stories or games to entertain their brothers, sisters, dolls, and animals. Sometimes rocks, empty cans, sticks or stones, and a great imagination are all girls need to have a wonderful time.

Japan

Cuba

Canada

United States

30

Puerto Rico

Chile

United States

Girls love games. Some games have been around for hundreds of years, even though their names and rules are different from country to country. You might enjoy making figures out of string, rope, or grass. In the United States girls call this game cat's cradle, and in Chile they play a game called *kai kai*. You might jump rope or play games like London Bridge, ring-around-the-rosy, or tug-of-war no matter where you live. Girls also love to play tag. In Argentina they enjoy *el gato y el ratôn* (cat and mouse), and in England they play British bulldog.

Colombia

Girls are strategic. Games like chess, billiards, and backgammon require deep concentration. Girls excel at these games because they know how to plan ahead. Jacks, hopscotch, marbles, and Ping-Pong require girls to be focused as well as coordinated, flexible, and quick. As more girls learn about computers, electronic games are becoming more popular. Many new Web sites have been developed to meet girls' interests.

Cuba

United States

Mexico

Girls are active. Some girls do exercises in school as part of their physical education classes. Others play at recess or during their lunch break. Girls also take part in organized sports and often practice after school or on weekends. Sometimes girls are discouraged from participating in sports. For many girls, recreation of any kind is considered a luxury that conflicts with school and chores. Other girls are not allowed to be physically active because of their cultural traditions. Even in the United States, few sports were available to girls thirty years ago. Today many girls start playing sports when they are very young. Often they become good enough to earn athletic scholarships to college.

United States

China

Japan

Girls are competitive. Some girls enjoy team sports, such as soccer, basketball, and volleyball, because they teach leadership and cooperation. Other girls prefer individual sports, such as skiing, running, gymnastics, or martial arts. All sports require commitment and practice, and they teach you about doing your best, regardless of whether you win or lose.

United States

Guinea

Sonya Bell

Sonya

Girls are pioneers. Sonya Bell, a teenager from the United States, is an all-around athlete. Being blind has not stopped her from achieving her dreams. As a runner, a gymnast, and an ice-skater, Sonya has received many medals, awards, and letters of recognition for her athletic accomplishments. Competing in a statewide high school track-and-field championship meet made Sonya a pioneer. Running track is her favorite sport, and she feels she owes her success to her faith and her determination. Sonya says, "All it takes to be a good competitor is courage, belief in yourself, and a positive attitude."

Nhemia Velasco

Girls are winners. Nhemia Velasco, from the Philippines, started swimming at age three. By age ten she held 132 gold medals from different competitions. Nhemia, or Em-Em, dreams of becoming the first Filipino to win an Olympic gold medal, and she trains several hours a day. This routine is all a part of achieving her goals. Her role model is Australian swimmer Dawn Fraser, who became a legend by winning events in three consecutive Olympic Games. According to Em-Em, "It takes a lot of hard work to do what I am doing, but the sacrifices are worth it. I want all kids to be involved in sports."

United States

Girls are athletes. You can play sports just for fun or train for many years. If you dream of being a great athlete, champions like track-and-field star Jackie Joyner-Kersee, ice-skaters Michelle Kwan and Lu Chen, soccer player Mia Hamm, golfer Se Ri Pak, basketball player Rebecca Lobo, and tennis stars Venus Williams and Serena Williams are inspiring role models.

China

Girls are trailblazers. Traditionally, ice hockey was a sport dominated by men. Today girls and women play this action-packed game. Many female ice hockey players were pioneers, playing with boys until girls' teams were formed. The courageous women's team from the United States won the 1998 Olympic gold medal in ice hockey. They proved that teamwork and determination can lead to victories as well as to lasting friendships.

Canada vs. China

India

France

Philippines

United States

Girls are strong. Through sports and play, you can become more confident as you test yourself in new ways. You build a healthy body that can leap, bend, twist, kick, flip, hit, and catch. You explore your creativity and build your imagination. As you grow up, you may discover that these activities have helped you become a focused young woman.

Mexico

Australia

Colombia

Friendship

Girls make wonderful friends. They find friends at school, on their sports teams, or through community activities. In the Igbo culture of Nigeria, friends may belong to the same *ogbo,* a group of girls and boys who play together, do their chores together, and give each other support. Like girls in the same *ogbo,* friends might live in the same neighborhood, or they might live on opposite sides of the world. Chat rooms on the Internet connect girls from Australia to Israel to Russia to the United States. Pen pals send letters that circle the globe. But no matter where girls live or what culture they belong to, their friendships have a lot in common.

Girls are fun. Whether they are playing at the park, dancing together, celebrating a birthday, eating ice cream, or helping each other with their homework, girls love to spend time together. You may eat lunch with your friends at school, go to the movies, or share secrets on the phone. Sleeping over at a friend's house can be an adventure. You can tell scary stories, read magazines, make up songs, eat junk food, and talk late into the night. Your conversations can go anywhere from boys to your favorite actors to the latest books and music.

Cuba

United States

Girls' friendships are magical. Around the world girls share their deepest problems and biggest dreams with their friends. Friends are the first you tell when something great happens—or when something goes wrong. They know just what to say to cheer you on or cheer you up. Sometimes you can tell what your friends are thinking or feeling without even being told.

Ethiopia

Friendships can also be tough. Sometimes you may feel excluded from different groups. You can also have big arguments with your very best friends, and you may even stop speaking for a while. But when a friendship is important, you find ways to work things out. Girls take time to talk and listen.

Vietnam

Spain

Maiamond

Maia Conçalves Fortes   Cathy Leathers

Girls are collaborative. Third, fourth, and fifth graders at Forest View Elementary School in Durham, North Carolina, in the United States, were part of the Girls' Advisory Team (GAT). Nineteen girls from five different countries and diverse backgrounds got together to play games, tell stories, create art, and share their experiences. They didn't know each other very well at first, but they became good friends over their many months together.

Girls are innovative. To express their commonalities and differences, the GAT members made pieces of life-size artwork called Girl Power Pals. Christina Quintano and Bora Kim created Bortina, who wears cool clothes, likes math and art, and has attitude and style. Liza Lehew and Kendra Lloyd created Lizkendel, who loves wearing crazy shirts, reading, playing soccer, and shopping at the mall with her friends.

Bortina

Bora Kim   Christina Quintano

Lizkendel

Liza Lehew   Kendra Lloyd

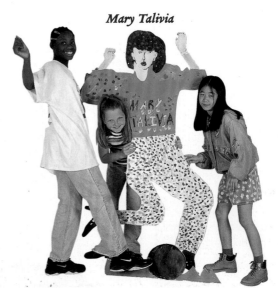

Mary Talivia

Tearra Smith   Mary Grace McGivney   Olivia Su

Feilicia

Jeena

Sarami

Fei Chi   *Alicia Oas*

Anna Sharpe   *Jenny Foreman*

Sara Dodson   *Asami Yokoyama*

Girls are spunky. Fei Chi and Alicia Oas created Feilicia, whose favorite subject is art. She loves wearing her shiny, sparkling blue jeans. Creating their Girl Power Pals gave the GAT members the chance to get to know each other better. Maia Conçalves Fortes says, "Friends share with each other love, happiness, sadness, play, and everything else."

Girls are loving. The greatest joys of friendship sometimes come from sharing your last scoop of ice cream with a good friend or walking home from school in the rain and making big splashes in mud puddles. Girls hold each other, laugh and cry together, work and play together, and stand strong together. Girls simply love each other.

Uganda

Guatemala

United States

Keepsakes

In this season be of daring spirit
behold the world from mountain peaks
Fuji, Everest, or Kilimanjaro.
Imagine hands on your hips, the wind
like hot breath on your brow.
You are regal.

Venture boldly into your dreams—
ride magenta winds through
Paris sky, paint the clouds a
lilac shade of purple,
if you like.

United States

In this season gather these gifts
of your springtime, dandelions,
sweet blades of grass,
wildflowers by the schoolhouse,
the dance of light in trees.

Seek often your own reflection
in mirrors and still streams,
embrace it like the morning sun,
caress it like black silk of night,

your graceful and agile limbs,
lips curved into a smile—
a crescent moon,
buoyant eyes like twinkling stars.

Keep memoirs of warm hugs,
your mama's cooking,
skipping to the corner shop with
friends, holding hands and
laughing out loud.

Honduras

In this morning of life
celebrate your immaculate self,
honor it in all your seasons to come.

—*Olateju Omolodun*

Afterword

Intense. Insightful. Energetic. Three women with a strong commitment to girls. Three individuals with different backgrounds, a common vision, and the persistence to be unstoppable. We are: a social entrepreneur and writer raised in eastern North Carolina; a poet and artistic performer born in Nigeria and brought up in North Carolina; and a health care leader and activist raised in suburban Chicago.

While none of us is an academic expert on girlhood, we each had our own joyous, painful, and challenging experiences as girls. We embarked on this book with a desire to celebrate girlhood around the world. We never realized how complex this project would become or that it would bring us face to face with some difficult questions: What does it mean to be a girl? How do families, friends, the media, and society shape girls' identities? How can we reconcile the joys of girlhood with painful realities like teenage pregnancy, eating disorders, lack of educational opportunities, and a tendency to undervalue girls wherever they live?

The most compelling question we faced was, how can society nurture the spirit, power, and strengths of all girls around the world? Through our research, we discovered that many girls are finding their own answers. Anthropologist Margaret Mead once said, "Never doubt that a small group of committed citizens can change the world. Indeed, it is the only thing that ever has." Girls everywhere are taking those words to heart.

The stories and photographs in this book highlight the richness, colors, talents, and beauty of girls everywhere. These images reflect the amazing diversity of girls in each country and around the world. We see parts of our own girlhoods in this book, and we hope that every girl who reads it finds herself here as well.

Maya Ajmera, age 8

Olateju Omolodun, age 8

Sarah Strunk, age 8

Spain

United States

Japan

Burkina Faso

Brazil

Thailand

Ecuador

El Salvador

Somalia

Ivory Coast

Arctic Ocean

Iceland

Canada

Irelar
United Kingo
Fran
Spa
Portug

North Atlantic Ocean

North Pacific Ocean

Morocc

United States

Mexico

Cuba

Puerto Rico

Jamaica

Guatemala · Honduras

Burkir
Faso

Guinea

Grenada

El Salvador

Liberia

Ivory
Coast

Colombia

Ghana

EQUATOR

Ecuador

Peru

Brazil

South Pacific Ocean

Bolivia

Chile

South Atlantic Ocean

Web Sites for Girls

Girls' Place, www.girlsplace.com

Girl Power!, www.health.org/gpower

Girl Power, www.girlpower.com

Girl Talk, www.livezone.com/girltalk

Girl Tech, www.girltech.com

A Girl's World, www.agirlsworld.com

Purple Moon, www.purple-moon.com

World Kids' Network, www.worldkids.net

Web Sites for Parents and Educators

Expect the Best from a Girl, www.academic.org

American Library Association's List of Great Sites for Children www.ala.org/parentspage/greatsites/arts2.html

Girl World: Take Our Daughters to Work Day, www.ms.foundation.org

Organizations

Boys and Girls Clubs of America, National Headquarters, 1230 West Peachtree Street, NW, Atlanta, GA 30309. Phone: 404-815-5700. Web site: www.bgca.org

Cambridge Female Education Trust (CamFed), 25 Wordsworth Grove, Cambridge CB3 9HH, United Kingdom. Phone: 44-1223-362648. Web site: www.camfed.org

Canadian Association of Girls in Science (CAGIS), University of Western Ontario, London, Ontario, Canada, N6A 5C1. Phone: 519-661-4029. Web site: www.uwo.ca/letstalkscience/CAGIS

Children's Defense Fund, National Headquarters, 25 E Street NW, Washington, DC 20001. Phone: 202-628-8787. Web site: www.childrensdefense.org

Children for a Safe Environment, 517 East Roanoke, Apt. 1, Phoenix, AZ 85004. Phone: 602-279-5001.

Girl Games/Planet Girl, 221 East 9th Street, Suite 302, Austin, TX 78701. Phone: 888-GRLS-RUL. Web site: www.planetgirl.com

Girls Incorporated, 120 Wall Street, 3rd Floor, New York, NY 10005. Phone: 212-509-2000. Web site: www.girlsinc.org

Girls Scouts of the U.S.A., 420 Fifth Avenue, New York, NY 10018. Phone: 212-852-8000. Web site: www.girlscouts.org

International Network for Girls, UNICEF NGO Committee, 3 UN Plaza, TA-24A, New York, NY 10017. Phone: 212-824-6394. Web site: www.girlsrights.org

The Kids' Hospital Network, P.O. Box 533, Harwich, MA 02645. Web site: www.bearabletimes.org

The Lewis Preston Fund for Girls' Education of the Global Fund for Women, 425 Sherman Avenue, Suite 300, Palo Alto, CA 94306. Phone: 650-853-8305. Web site: www.globalfundforwomen.org

Seeds of Peace, 370 Lexington Avenue, Suite 1409, New York, NY 10017. Phone: 212-573-8046. Web site: www.seedsofpeace.org

Sisterhood Agenda, 3308 Chapel Hill Boulevard, Suite 133, Durham, NC 27707. Phone: 919-493-8358.

Suitcases for Kids, c/o Aubyn Burnside, P.O. Box 1144, Hickory, NC 28603.

Women's Sports Foundation, Eisenhower Park, East Meadow, NY 11554. Phone: 800-227-3988. Web site: www.lifetimetv.com/WoSport

YWCA of the U.S.A., Empire State Building, Suite 301, 350 Fifth Avenue, New York, NY 10118. Phone: 212-273-7800. Web site: www.ywca.org

United States

Thailand

45

Acknowledgments

Financial support for this project has been provided by the Arthur M. Blank Family Foundation, The Body Shop USA, the Ford Foundation, Girl's Best Friend Foundation, the Nokomis Foundation, the Grace Jones Richardson Trust, the Unity Avenue Foundation, the Women's Sports Foundation, and Friends of _Extraordinary Girls_.

Deepest thanks to Kelly Swanson, our editor at Charlesbridge Publishing, for challenging us every step of the way. She has truly gone above and beyond the role of editor, and her spirit and passion are reflected in this book, too. As always, special thanks to Anne Theilgard of Kachergis Book Design for embracing our vision—time and time again.

We received over 10,000 captivating images of girls from around the world. We wish we could have included all of them. We are so grateful to all of the photographers who believed in the vision and value of this project, and we appreciate their patience in this partnership. Quite simply, without their photographs there would be no book.

Our heartfelt thanks to Girls Incorporated® for their belief in and support of this project. A special thank you to Isabel Carter Stewart for her inspirational foreword and to Heather Johnston Nicholson, Nancy Smith, Galia Schechter, and Andrea Nemetz. Thank you to Scott Griffin of Ida Rankin Elementary School, Kavita Ramdas of the Global Fund for Women, and Anita Roddick of The Body Shop for their words of praise and enthusiasm.

We are grateful to Jill McLean Taylor of Simmons College and Bill Young of Westminster College for their insightful comments. We also appreciate our many reviewers, translators, and focus groups for their assistance and feedback. We are indebted to Jacqueline Geschickter, special projects editor of _National Geographic World_ magazine, who introduced us to many of the girls and organizations featured in this book. In addition, special thanks to Church World Service, International Art Publishers, and World Vision.

A cornerstone of the philosophy behind **SHAKTI** for Children's books is the integration of the child's voice in our work. To that end, we thank the Girls' Advisory Team at Forest View Elementary School in Durham, North Carolina, for their creativity, insight, and honesty, and for helping us to develop the vision of _Extraordinary Girls_. Thanks to GAT members Fei Chi, Diamond Conrad, Sara Dodson, Jenny Foreman, Maia Conçalves Fortes, Jasmine Jones, Margaret Jones, Cathy Leathers, Liza Lehew, Kendra Lloyd, Bora Kim, Mary Grace McGivney, Alicia Oas, Christina Quintano, Anna Sharpe, Erin Shaw, Tearra Smith, Olivia Su, and Asami Yokoyama, as well as to Forest View art teacher Marylu Flowers and principal Toni Hill.

Special thanks to our colleagues at the Global Fund for Children: Katie Bell, Lucy Melvin, and Cathy Nichols, and to the Fund's board of directors: William Ascher, David Edward, Laura Luger, Carol O'Brien, and Adele Richardson Ray.

Extraordinary Girls is a project of **SHAKTI** for Children, which is dedicated to teaching children to value diversity. **SHAKTI** for Children is a program of the Global Fund for Children: www.globalfundforchildren.org

Details about the donation of royalties can be obtained by writing to Charlesbridge Publishing and the Global Fund for Children at the addresses below.

Developed by **SHAKTI** for Children
The Global Fund for Children
1612 K Street N.W., Suite 706, Washington, D.C. 20006
(202) 331-9003
www.shakti.org

Published by Charlesbridge Publishing
85 Main Street, Watertown, MA 02472
(617) 926-0329
www.charlesbridge.com

Library of Congress Cataloging-in-Publication Data
Ajmera, Maya.
Extraordinary Girls/Maya Ajmera, Olateju Omolodun, and Sarah Strunk; foreword by Isabel Carter Stewart.
p.   cm.
Summary: Emphasizes the qualities, abilities, and achievements of girls from different countries and cultures around the world.
     ISBN 0-88106-065-8 (reinforced for library use)
     ISBN 0-88106-066-6 (softcover)
1. Girls—Juvenile literature. 2. Girls—Cross-cultural studies—Juvenile literature. 3. Success in children—Juvenile literature. [1. Girls. 2. Self-realization. 3. Individuality.] I. Omolodun, Olateju. II. Strunk, Sarah. III. Title.
HQ777.A66   1999
305.23—dc21   98-46146

(hc) 10 9 8 7 6 5 4 3
(sc) 10 9 8 7 6 5 4 3 2

This book was separated, printed, and bound by Pacifica Communications, Inc., South Korea.

Text and jacket design by Kachergis Book Design, Pittsboro, NC

Other **SHAKTI** for Children/Charlesbridge Books
Children from Australia to Zimbabwe: A Photographic Journey around the World by Maya Ajmera and Anna Rhesa Versola
Let the Games Begin by Maya Ajmera and Michael J. Regan
To Be a Kid by Maya Ajmera and John Ivanko
Xanadu, the Imaginary Place: A Showcase of Writings and Artwork by North Carolina's Children edited by Maya Ajmera and Olateju Omolodun

Finland

Creative

Scientific

Competitive

Inquisitive

Loving

Artistic

Compassionate

Caring

Courageous

Curious

Musical

Fun

Active

Expressive

Strong